PRAYERS

for a

PRIVILEGED

PEOPLE

WALTER BRUEGGEMANN

PRAYERS
for a
PRIVILEGED
PEOPLE

Abingdon Press
Nashville

PRAYERS FOR A PRIVILEGED PEOPLE

Copyright © 2008 by Abingdon Press

All rights reserved.

This book is printed on acid-free paper.

Library of Congress Cataloging-in-Publication Data

Brueggemann, Walter.
    Prayers for a privileged people / Walter Brueggemann.
        p. cm.
    Includes bibliographical references and index.
    ISBN 978-0-687-65019-4 (binding: pbk. with lay-flat binding : alk. paper)
    1. Americans—Prayers and devotions.   2. United States—Prayers and devotions.
3. Prayers. I. Title.

BR517.B78 2008
242'.8--dc22

2007038978

08 09 10 11 12 13 14 15 16 17—10 9 8 7 6 5 4 3 2 1

MANUFACTURED IN THE UNITED STATES OF AMERICA

I am glad to dedicate this book to my new grandson,
Peter William Brueggemann,
who, like many of us, is born into some privilege
and invited to a life of reflection, yielding,
and glad obedience.

Contents

CONTENTS

Section 4: Brick Production

Section 5: Can We Risk It?

CONTENTS

CONTENTS

Preface

Prayers "for privileged people" isn't a new idea to me, primarily because I am inordinately privileged in every way . . . white, male, tenured, blessed with every gift our political economy could provide. Thus it is no challenge for me to rethink myself along with other privileged believers, even if our privilege tends to work against openheartedness. To think, imagine, and verbalize prayer in such a company—for most of the churches where I worship are exactly such venues of privilege—means that these prayers are more or less context specific. Well, all prayer is context specific, whether recognized as such or not. We pray as bodied selves in bodied communities, and we cannot pray otherwise, for most of the secrets we do not hide from God arise with context specificity. In such an imagined environment, it is inescapable that hard issues like privilege and entitlement, injustice and violence would be on the table.

Even though these prayers were accumulated over time in a random, ad hoc way—variously evoked by circumstance—the organization of the prayers in this collection is itself a quite conscious decision about the field of such prayers. Indeed, the six sections of this collection together trace in a direct way the contours of prayer that begin in self-awareness and end in glad yielding to the goodness of God.

The first section plays upon the "Collect for Purity" that begins many worship services in liturgical tradition. That prayer itself is a yielding of self to God, the expression of our awareness that entry into the presence of God depends upon God's gracious, transformative action toward us. Entry into God's presence is not to be done lightly or easily, but with great intentionality concerning the incommensurate partnership of communion with God.

The collection moves toward a reflection on the well-ordered, well-arranged, even "blessed" lives of well-being that belong to those of us who are privileged culturally, politically, and economically. Such reflection is regularly enacted and dramatized in "set occasions" when the right working of our lives is celebrated and legitimated in quite public ways. These prayers reflect on such occasions of legitimation when our privilege in the world is given religious endorsement. However, they also reflect the idea that along with our joy and thankfulness, we recognize in our moments of candor the gap between the privileged and the not-so-privileged.

Our well-ordered legitimacy is not guaranteed. We are aware, even amid our gratitude for well-being, that our "safe worlds" are profoundly under threat and that anxiety is not inappropriate amid the daily round of our common life. These prayers ponder the reality of threat among us, the attraction of power and control in contrast to the vulnerability that belongs to the God disclosed in Jesus of Nazareth. The mismatch between our thirst for security, the reality of insecurity, and the "weakness" of God converges in an act of self-recognition.

When we think and notice and pray beyond ourselves, we are mindful of many others who do not participate with us in that privilege. There are those all around us who live lives of deficit and need, who are cut off from power, denied access to the gains of our society, and who face daily vulnerability. They are not automatically or everywhere a threat to our comfort and privilege. But they are there, and they will not go away. As we are haunted by them, so they inhabit our prayers. We are wont to regard them as an inconvenience, if not a threat. But we know, when we settle toward God's rule, that they are sisters and brothers who share with us a common destiny and a common mercy from God. We are not able, by our will or intellect, to disengage from them. And so we pray for them and, when we are able, we pray alongside them.

As we acknowledge our privilege, name our anxieties, and recognize our brothers and sisters, we are surprised by a call from

God. Rather than autonomous agents of self-regard in the world, we are gifted by, belong with, and answer to another. This other, the Holy One, sends our life off in new directions . . . out beyond our privilege. Thus, such prayer is a summons to get our minds off ourselves, to ponder the God who gives us life, and who dispatches us for the sake of the lives of others.

As we go to the places where we are called by God—sometimes gladly, sometimes reluctantly, always in anxiety—we are drawn into the newness of God's future. We do not, as we are drawn there, settle into cages of isolation and despair. Rather, our lives are resituated in a chorus of possibilities. We have glimpses of Easter newness. As we trust ourselves to that glimpse, we find gifts of newness all around. Those gifts in turn propel us to self-abandoning wonder, love, and praise. By the time we finish our prayers, we have yielded in gladness and become other than we were, carriers of hope that will not quit, refusing any longer the closed reality of status quo.

It is evident that such a drama of acknowledgment and yielding that constitutes prayer is, in effect, a subversive activity. It is a refusal to accept in passive ways the closed, fixed world of privilege that wants us to exclude others and deny God's future that insistently destabilizes our present tense. Every time we pray, we engage in such a subversive activity and thereby align ourselves with the Easter power of God that surges among us and invites us to a different way in the world. It is no obvious or "natural" matter to resituate our lives with reference to the holy power and purpose of God. But that is what we do in prayer. And when we pray, we find our hearts opened, our secrets exposed, and our desires known. We arrive at a readiness to love God perfectly and to magnify God's name in the world. It is my hope that these prayers will be useful and faithful resources for the kind of glad yielding now so urgent among us.

It remains for me to thank John Kutsko, who initiated this project. Thanks also to Tia Foley, who worked from my scratched prayers to make them legible and coherent for the editors. I am grateful to them and to the company of the privileged who have prayed along with me.

SECTION 1

Opening Our Hearts: The Collect

Prayer is an act of openness to the One
who sits on the throne of mercy.
When we pray, we participate in the
ultimate practice of humanness as we yield
to a Power greater than ourselves.
Our best prayers engage in candor about
our lives, practice vulnerability, run risks,
and rest in confident trust.

Unto Whom All Hearts Are Open

The pastor says, "Almighty God, unto whom all hearts are open . . ."
   We rush to the next phrase,
        but now we linger there.
   We ponder our hearts . . .
        our deepest feelings of love and devotion,
        our closest organ of vitality,
        our place of deep decision-making,
        our instrument of being fully ourselves.

Our hearts—that throb for contact with you—
   our hearts are open.
   They are not always open by our choice,
     for we would like sometimes to
        close our hearts and our minds and our hands.
   But they are open, because
     our hearts cannot resist
     your steady care and address.
   Our hearts are open for you, very God.
     You are the one who has made us
        so that our hearts are restless
        till they rest in you.

Do your mysterious, majestic God-ing
   with our hearts:
        reclaim,
        renew,
        re-enliven,
   that we may leave your presence
        transplanted,
        transformed,
        transposed,

become by your attentiveness whom we
        have not yet embraced,
    open and receptive,
    honest and undefensive,
    unafraid and committed to obedience.

Let the pulse of our heart throb now,
    according to the cadences of your rule;
    command and we will obey,
    overrule and we will yield,
    lead and we will walk
            where we never thought to go.

Unto you . . .
    not unto each other,
    not unto our pet projects,
    not unto our favorite charity or passion.
Unto you . . . our hearts are open;
    we are yours; be our God—yet again.

All Desires Are Known

The leader says, "Almighty God, unto whom . . . all desires are
        known."
  We rush to the next phrase,
      but now linger there.
We are creatures inhabited by many desires.
  When we hear the word "desire,"
      we first of all think of sex,
    and we are propelled by such sexuality
        that you have called good but that we fear and distort.
    But some of us are shriveled in sexuality
      and can scarce remember desire.

But the word "desire" reaches deep and wide:
  Some of us have traded off sex for money
      and we can never have enough;
  Some of us are so anxious and we desire
      most of all control, to have control,
        to be in control;
  Some of us are so full of hate and resentment,
     that we desire most of all to see our
         enemies overwhelmed:
             an old sibling threat,
             an alienated lover,
             a rival, a competitor,
             an Arab, a Jew,
             a Communist, a gay person.

We spend our energy managing our desires,
    waiting on them, investing in them, keeping them hidden.
But you know, and you know by your presence how to change our
        desires,
  because in your presence,

our desires lose their power
as we receive again your look of love,
your powerful embrace,
your steady summons,
and then we know our desires
are all too self-indulgent,
interrupted by the precious psalmist,
"Whom have I in heaven but you?
And there is nothing on earth that
I desire other than you."

You have made us to desire only you,
you, our beginning and our end,
you, our food and our rest,
you, our joy and our peace.

Turn us from our desires that obsess us.
Unburden us that we may know
our true desire and end in communion with you,
you, who desire us as companion and lover.

From Whom No Secrets Are Hid

The priest says, "Almighty God . . . from whom no secrets are
    hid."
    We rush to the next phrase but now linger there.
We are rich conundrums of secrets,
    we weave a pattern of lies in order to be
                    well thought of,
    we engage in subterfuge about our truth.
We carry old secrets too painful to utter,
                    too shameful to acknowledge,
                    too burdensome to bear,
    of failures we cannot undo,
    of alienations we regret but cannot fix,
    of grandiose exhibits we cannot curb.
And you know them.
    You know them all.
    And so we take a deep sigh in your presence,
        no longer needing to pretend and
                    cover up and
                    deny.

We mostly do not have big sins to confess,
    only modest shames that do not
        fit our hoped-for selves.

And then we find that *your knowing* is more
    powerful than *our secrets.*
You know and do not turn away,
    and our secrets that seemed too powerful
        are emptied of strength,
    secrets that seemed too burdensome
            are now less severe.

We marvel that when you find us out
      you stay with us,
   taking us seriously,
   taking our secrets soberly,
      but not ultimately,
   overpowering our little failure
   with your massive love
            and abiding patience.

We long to be fully, honestly
      exposed to your gaze of gentleness.
   In the moment of your knowing
            we are eased and lightened,
   and we feel the surge of joy move in our bodies,
      because we are not *ours* in cringing
            but *yours* in communion.

We are yours and find the truth before you
   makes us free for
      wonder, love, and praise—and new life.

Cleanse the Thoughts

Every time we meet,
   we pray that you would "cleanse the thoughts of
      our hearts by the inspiration of thy Holy Spirit."

We present ourselves for that strange interface
   between our thoughts and your spirit.

We covet our thoughts that do not stay focused
      about getting out of church on time and
      errands to run after church and
      meals to purchase and folks to see;
   our thoughts reflect our excessive busyness
      that leaves us little time for our life with you.

And beneath busyness our thoughts are preoccupied
   with hopes that linger in disappointment,
   with hurts that refuse to be healed,
   with guilt that does not easily yield to pardon,
   with estrangements that cut deep and remain open,
   with can-do confidence about power and energy
           and achievement.

We think a thousand thoughts in a minute . . .
   of money and sex and control
      and loss and death and
         cell phones and loneliness
         and good food.

And then you . . .
   you who give light and wind and life,
   you who watch over us with sustaining power
      and disciplining presence;

you will us well and whole
and by stealth turn our lives in freshness.

We present ourselves,
seeking . . . grudgingly . . . that you will
equip us to relinquish thoughts that
we have thought too long and too often,
seeking that you will restore us to the joy of
your presence,
seeking that you will make things new
in our stale, weary lives.

What we seek, only you can give;
What we ask, we cannot find ourselves;
What we want is a gift
and the open graciousness to receive it
on your terms.
Come Holy Spirit!

Perfectly Love

We pray, as often as we meet,
   that we might "perfectly love you."
Indeed, we have been commanded from the beginning,
     to love you with all our hearts and
              all our souls and
              all our minds and
              all our strength.

We have pledged to love,
   pledged in our prayers and in our baptism,
     in our confirmation and with our best resolve.

But we confess . . .
   we love you imperfectly;
   we love you with a divided heart,
     with a thousand other loves
        that are more compelling,
     with reservation and qualification,
        and passion withheld and
           devotion impaired.

We do not now come to pretend before you,
   but to confess that we do not,
         as we are,
   love you perfectly;
       we do not keep your commands;
       we do not order our lives by your purpose;
       we do not tilt toward you as our deepest affection.

But we would . . .
   we would love you more perfectly,
     by the taste of bread become your flesh,

by the swallow of wine become your blood,
by the praise of our lips and beyond our usual reasoning,
by the commandments that are not burden but joy to us,
by embracing your passion for neighbors,
by your ways of justice and peace and mercy,
by honoring the world you have made
      and all creatures great and small,
by self-care that knows you as our creator.

Lead us past our shabby compromises
  and our cheap devotion;
lead us into singleness of vision
    and purity of heart,
    that we may will one thing,
and answer back in love to your great love to us.

Free us from idolatries,
    and our habits of recalcitrance,
    tender our hearts,
    gentle our lips,
    open our hands,
  that we may turn toward you fully
    toward your world unguardedly.

  Let us bask in your freedom
    to be fully yours, and
    so trusting fully our own.
We pray through the Lord Jesus who loved you
    singularly, perfectly, fully—to the end.

Worthily Magnify

We pray, as often as we meet,
    that we might "worthily magnify thy holy Name."
Except that before your holy name,
    we mumble in awe and timidity and cowardice.
    Your holy name we can hardly utter:
        the father of all orphans,
        the son who is crucified and risen,
        the spirit who blows where it will,
        creator, maker of all that is,
        redeemer, who frees us from the power of death,
        sanctifier who blesses us with betterness.

    Your holy name that causes powers to tremble
        and angels to yield.
    Your holy name that causes chaos to settle,
        and death to depart,
        and feverish anxiety to grow quiet.
    Your name we dare entertain in our dry mouths,
        on our thin tongues,
        between our quivering lips.

No, we are not worthy to utter your name,
    we are so anxious and devious,
    we are so preoccupied and distracted,
    we who cannot stay awake to watch with you one hour,
    we who have our own ways in the world that are not
        your ways.

Except you have entrusted your holy name to us;
    you have called us as your witnesses;
    you have empowered us to be your good news messengers.

So we pray in this awesome moment in your presence,
    match up your holy name with our poor testimony,
    that we may make your name and your power and your purpose
      very large and awesome and compelling,
    large before the rulers of this age,
    awesome amid the violence of
          our world and our government,
    compelling amid our mad pursuit of oil
      and commodities and safety.

We pray for freedom and courage to praise you,
    that by our praise,
      the angels in heaven may be invited to awe,
      the folk among us may be summoned to notice,
      the children in our midst may be moved to trust you.

You, you the lamb that is slain,
      are worthy to be praised.
  Take our unworthy selves
    and by your good power
        let our praise toward you be done worthily.

That you, your kingdom and your power and your glory
        may be made large
        in our times and
        in our places,
        here and now—made very large.

SECTION 2

Well-Arranged Lives

We are a people of privilege and
entitlement. We are among the *haves*—
we have education, connections, power,
and wealth. Too often we are indulgent
and self-sufficient consumers. We speak of
our achievements and accomplishments.
Sometimes we offer God liturgies of
disregard, litanies of selves made too
big. But we hear faint reminders of a
better way.

Our Charter of Entitlement

We are mostly the kind of people who do well and
                    who mean well.
We know how to do what must be done and
        we get up and do it.

We have a sense of our worth and our capacity to perform.
We care for our children and our futures
                    and our good schools.
    And after good schools come college
        and learning and degree and profession
                    and security.

We sit in and enjoy our responsible entitlement that we have
                    surely earned.
    But along with success and well-being,
        we wish our children happy,
        so we protect and extend adolescence;
        we build barriers against ugliness and failure,
            and struggle with too much work and stress.

We have and treasure all the signs of entitlement,
            all the props of affluence,
            all the symbols of well-being.
How peculiar that we have it all and worry about
        immigrants who might acquire some small part of our legacy.

In this moment of candor before you,
    we step into that gap in our life
        between assured entitlement and the threat of immigrants,
        between our indulgence of our children and
            the violence that mostly lacks shame.

Move us by your hovering that we may come to ourselves,
    that we may notice the ways in which we are
        far from home,
    that we may reckon how we have betrayed
        ourselves for quick fixes.

Give us the capacity to return to you,
    to be welcomed home,
    to be forgiven,
    to be invited to dance
        and then to a fatted calf,
        to receive it all as a gift from you.

As people of entitlement and violence, we converge with
                    immigrants,
    we learn together how deeply in need we are;
    receive us and move us that we may accept
        your welcome to newness.

Return us to innocence,
                even while we are frightened.

Exhibit to us your great simplicity among
                our complex habits.

Call us at last by our right names,
                because we are yours.

Close to Being Empty-Handed

We are among the builders,
        we do silos and missile silos,
        we do tall towers and large granaries,
        we do pyramids and monuments and
            steeples and high-rises,
        we build because we are able,
            because it looks good,
            because it feels good,
            because we have so
                much stuff to store
        we need bigger, better barns.

We make it tall and shiny and beautiful
   only to discover that moth and rust consume,
   only to discover that shiny surface turns empty shell,
   only to discover that storage is for goods
            that melt and sour.

We end closer to empty-handed than we imagined.

As we are able we turn from our cities to you,
          we turn from our successes to you,
          we turn from our reason to you,
          we turn from our power to you.
To you, to you, to you, to you,
   our help is in no other
     save in you alone.
You only, you enough, you in your generosity.

Whom have we in heaven but you? There is nothing on earth that we desire other than you.

Hear our trust and our thanks and our readiness to obey.

The Noise of Politics

We watch as the jets fly in
    with the power people and
    the money people,
    the suits, the budgets, the billions.

We wonder about monetary policy
    because we are among the haves,
and about generosity
    because we care about the have-nots.

By slower modes we notice
   Lazarus and the poor arriving from Africa,
   and the beggars from Central Europe, and
   the throng of environmentalists
    with their vision of butterflies and oil
        of flowers and tanks
        of growing things and
          killing fields.

We wonder about peace and war,
    about ecology and development,
    about hope and entitlement.

We listen beyond jeering protesters and
    soaring jets and
   faintly we hear the mumbling of the crucified one,
   something about
    feeding the hungry
    and giving drink to the thirsty,
    about clothing the naked,
    and noticing the prisoners,
    more about the least and about holiness among them.

We are moved by the mumbles of the gospel,
   even while we are tenured in our privilege.

We are half ready to join the choir of hope,
         half afraid things might change,
            and in a third half of our faith
               turning to you,
            and your outpouring love
            that works justice and
            that binds us each and all to one another.

So we pray amid jeering protesters
      and soaring jets.
   Come by here and make new,
      even at some risk to our entitlements.

The State of the Union

We will watch and listen tonight for the State of the Union
        message:
  We will hear as the Sergeant of Arms says dramatically,
    "Mr. Speaker, the President of the United States."
  We will watch the choreographed procession down the
    aisle with much backslapping, applause, and good humor;
  We will all be there:
    the leading military people,
    the chief justice,
    the senate leader,
    the house leader,
    no doubt a few momentary "heroes" in the balcony.

We will listen to hear that the union is in good shape:
  the war is being won;
  the economy is coming back;
  migrants are facing new rigors;
  unemployment is down.

There will be much applause—
  and we will be glad for such political performance.

Except, of course, we know better.
  For this is not an assembly of the union,
  this is a gathering of "the suits,"
  the men—and some women—who have good educations
    and even better connections.
  It is a meeting of wealth, and entitlement, and privilege.

We will watch and notice with some wistfulness
  all of those who are absent from the meeting:
    the poor who lack voice,

the pensioners who lack health coverage,
the unemployed who lack benefits,
the gays who still live under threat,
the victims of disasters who still need our help,
the prisoners who live at the very edge of
      their constitutional rights.

We will embrace the buoyancy of the speech with gladness
    and with great dis-ease,
  because we know better.
  We know better because our Lord has told us about
    the lame and the blind,
    the hungry, the homeless, the poor,
    the prisoners, the ones who thirst.
And we are in touch, by our baptism, with them.

We hope and pray and work for a more perfect union,
  a binding of all by dignity and security and well-being,
    and less binding by money and connections and power.

Our Lord is so weak and so foolish and so poor,
  and yet he is our Savior.
We are pulled apart by our double awareness
  of self-satisfaction and dis-ease.
We submit to your goodness our vexed lives
  that we cannot resolve.
Give us honesty and openness that we may become aware
  of the true state of our union.

Super Bowl Sunday

The world of fast money,
    and loud talk,
    and much hype is upon us.
    We praise huge men whose names will linger only briefly.

We will eat and drink,
    and gamble and laugh,
    and cheer and hiss,
    and marvel and then yawn.

We show up, most of us, for such a circus,
        and such an indulgence.
    Loud clashing bodies,
    violence within rules,
    and money and merchandise and music.

And you—today like every day—
    you govern and watch and summon;
    you glad when there is joy in the earth,
    But you notice our liturgies of disregard and
        our litanies of selves made too big,
        our fascination with machismo power,
            and lust for bodies and for big bucks.

And around you gather today, as every day,
    elsewhere uninvited, but noticed acutely by you,
        those disabled and gone feeble,
        those alone and failed,
        those uninvited and shamed.
And you whose gift is more than "super,"
    overflowing, abundant, adequate, all sufficient.

The day of preoccupation with creature comforts writ large.
We pause to be mindful of our creatureliness,
  our commonality with all that is small and vulnerable exposed,
  your creatures called to obedience and praise.

Give us some distance from the noise,
  some reserve about the loud success of the day,
  that we may remember that our life consists
    not in things we consume
    but in neighbors we embrace.

Be our good neighbor that we may practice
  your neighborly generosity all through our needy
      neighborhood.

Marked by Ashes

Ruler of the Night, Guarantor of the Day . . .
This day—a gift from you.
This day—like none other you have ever given,
    or we have ever received.
This Wednesday dazzles us with gift and newness and possibility.
This Wednesday burdens us with the tasks of the day,
    for we are already halfway home
                halfway back to committees and memos,
                halfway back to calls and appointments,
                halfway on to next Sunday,
                halfway back, half frazzled, half expectant,
                half turned toward you, half rather not.

This Wednesday is a long way from Ash Wednesday,
    but all our Wednesdays are marked by ashes—
        we begin this day with that taste of ash in our mouth:
            of failed hope and broken promises,
            of forgotten children and frightened women,
            of more war casualties, more violence, more cynicism;
        we ourselves are ashes to ashes,
                dust to dust;
        we can taste our mortality as we roll the ash around
            on our tongues.

We are able to ponder our ashness with
    some confidence, only because our every Wednesday of ashes
    anticipates your Easter victory over that dry, flaky taste
        of death.

On this Wednesday, we submit our ashen way to you—
    you Easter parade of newness.
    Before the sun sets, take our Wednesday and Easter us,

Easter us to joy and energy and courage and freedom;
Easter us that we may be fearless for your truth.
Come here and Easter our Wednesday with
mercy and justice and peace and generosity.

We pray as we wait for the Risen One who comes soon.

Sustained by Angels

On reading Mark 1:12-13

Maybe we have not thought much about Satan,
   either in glib self-regard,
   or in rejection of such silly speculation,
   or in a way more urbane and benign
      than to imagine such a character.

Except that as we begin our strenuous Lenten trek,
   we are aware
      that the power of resistance is at work in our midst,
      that the force of negation is alive and well,
      that our best will is contradicted
         by stuff that surges
            against our best selves,
      that we, even we, are prone to our
         several addictions that render us helpless.

So we pray in the Lenten season,
   give us primitive freedom to
      take full stock of Satan and the power of
      evil still among us in our prosperity and
      wealth and sophistication,
   and give us primitive openness
      to your ministering angels
         who are present with care and gentleness
            and great nourishment.

In the Lenten season, give us freedom
   to reconfigure our lives
      as a testing field between the force of Satan
         and the food of your angels.

Enter our lives with power for newness,
   deliver us from a sense of naive mastery,
   and give us honest contact with our vulnerability.

Enter the deep places of our life and claim us for your purposes.
We would be more free than we are,
   more bold than we dare,
   more obedient than we choose.

We wait for the gift of your large gift of life
   that will wrench us away from death
      to the miracle of Easter joy.

Candidates for Newness

We live the long stretch between
   Easter and Pentecost, scarcely noticing.
We hear mention of the odd claim of ascension.
We easily recite the creed,
   "He ascended into heaven."
We bow before such quaint language and move on,
   immune to ascent,
   indifferent to enthronement,
   unresponsive to new governance.

It is reported that behind the ascending son was
   the majestic Father riding the clouds,
   But we do not look up much;
     we stay close to the ground, to business and
         to busyness,
         to management and control.

Our world of well-being has a very low
   ceiling, but we do not mind the closeness
     or notice the restrictiveness.
It will take at least a Pentecost wind to
   break open our vision enough to imagine new governance.

We will regularly say the creed
   and from time to time—in crises that
        drive us to hope and to wish—
wait for a new descent of the spirit among us.

Until then, we stay jaded,
    but for all that,
        no less candidates for newness.

Blown by the Spirit . . .
We Know Not Where

We hear the story of the wind at Pentecost,
    Holy wind that dismantles what was,
    Holy wind that evokes what is to be,
    Holy wind that overrides barriers and causes communication,
    Holy wind that signals your rule even among us.

We are dazzled, but then—reverting to type—
    we wonder how to harness the wind,
        how to manage the wind by our technology,
        how to turn the wind to our usefulness,
        how to make ourselves managers of the wind.

Partly we do not believe such an odd tale
        because we are not religious freaks;
Partly we resist such a story,
        because it surges beyond our categories;
Partly we had imagined you to be more ordered
        and reliable than that.

So we listen, depart, and return to our ordered existence:
    we depart with only a little curiosity
            but not yielding;
    we return to how it was before,
        unconvinced but wistful, slightly praying for wind,
            craving for newness,
            wishing to have it all available to us.

We pray toward the wind and wait, unconvinced but wistful.

At Thanksgiving

Amid football,
     family, and
     too much food,
  we pause quickly and without inconvenience
     to remember and to thank.
     We remember ancient pilgrims
          who followed dreams of alabaster cities
               and financial opportunity;
     We remember hospitable first nation people
          who welcomed them, and then lost their land;
     We remember other family times
          filled with joy and
          filled with anxiety, and
               old scars still powerful.
     We thank you for this U.S. venue of
          justice and freedom,
          and are aware of its flawed reality;
     We thank you for our wealth and our safety,
          and are aware of how close to poverty we are
               and how under threat we live.

We gather our impulse for gratitude today,
   grateful to you and to our ancestors,
   grateful to you for our families,
                    our health,
                    our government,
                    our many possessions.

We gladly affirm that
   "All good gifts around us are sent from heaven above,"
   But we yield to none in a sense of self-sufficiency,
      our weariness in needing to share,
      our resentfulness of those who take and do not give.

Your generosity evokes our gratitude,
but your generosity overmatches our gratitude.
    We are ready to thank,
        but not overly so;
    We remember our achievements,
                our accomplishments,
                our entitlements,
                and our responsibilities
        that slice away our yielding of ourselves to you.

Move through our half measure of thanks
    and let us be, all through this day,
    more risky in acknowledging
        that we have nothing except what you give.

You have given so much—not least your only Son.
Gift us the gift of dazzlement and awe
    that we may rejoice in our penultimate lives
    and keep you ultimate all the day long,
        relishing the wonder of your self-giving love.

Newborn Beginning . . .
after Caesar

The Christ Child is about to be born,
 the one promised by the angel.
  Mary's "fullness of time" has arrived.
Except that the birth is scheduled
 according to the emperor:
 A decree went out that all should be numbered.

Caesar decreed a census, everyone counted;
Caesar intended to have up-to-date data for the tax rolls;
Caesar intended to have current lists of draft eligibility;
Caesar intended taxes to support armies,
 because the emperor, in whatever era,
  is always about money and power,
   about power and force,
   about force and control,
    and eventually violence.

And while we wait for the Christ Child,
 we are enthralled by the things of Caesar—
  money . . . power . . . control,
   and all the well-being that comes from
   such control, even if it requires a little violence.

But in the midst of the decree
 will come this long-expected Jesus,
  innocent, vulnerable,
  full of grace and truth,
  grace and not power,
  truth and not money,
  mercy and not control.

We also dwell in the land of Caesar;
  we pray for the gift of your spirit,
  that we may loosen our grip on the things of Caesar,
  that we may turn our eyes toward the baby,
        our ears toward the newness,
        our hearts toward the gentleness,
        our power and money and control
            toward your new governance.

We crave the newness.
  And while the decree of the emperor
    rings in our ears with such authority,
  give us newness that we may start again
        at the beginning,
  that the innocence of the baby may
        intrude upon our ambiguity,
  that the vulnerability of the child may
        veto our lust for control,
  that we may be filled with wonder
        and so less of anxiety,
    in the blessed name of the baby we pray.

Caesar's Imprint

On reading 1 Kings 12:1-18

We talk theology;
we breathe image, metaphor, abstraction;
we credit you with big acts of mercy
    and great strokes of judgment.
We are paid to live in the rarified air of faith.
  But after dark, out of the office,
  we follow the money as best we can;
  we worry about church contributions and pledges
      and budgets;
  we peek at our IRAs and pension funds;
  we worry about health care
    and college tuition.

We read our lives through the flat questions of Karl Marx,
  and so it does not surprise us that at Solomon's
    death, the issue of taxation came up.
  We watch the old, wise advisors to the king;
  we notice the young brash alternatives for the king;
  we observe the silly, foolish king,
    as his power and authority ebb away,
  and the kingdom falls apart.

We are indeed money creatures;
    we pay our taxes
      and fund war
      and hope for gentle welfare.

We pray about sins, but
  more often about debts to be forgiven
  and trespasses against the neighbor to be pardoned.

We come at you as bodied selves
    with food and sex and money on our minds.

Deliver us from too much theology,
    from too many images,
    from abstractions that are too rich,
    and too much conviction about things spiritual.

Give us courage and energy for the issues of
    taxation and poverty and welfare,
    and the fleeting chances for justice and compassion and mercy.

Our prayer is in the name of Jesus who
    watched the coins drop into the temple plate,
        and wondered about Caesar's imprint
            on our worth.

Sovereign

We name you king, Lord, sovereign.
    We trust you, except
        sometimes we do not.
        We take matters into our own hands.

We fashion power and authority and sovereignty;
    enforced by law and bureaucracy and weapons,
        we think to make ourselves safe.
    And then learn, staggeringly,
        how insufficient is our product,
        how thin is our law,
        how ineffective is our bureaucracy,
        how impotent our weapons.

We are driven back to you—your will,
                          your purpose,
                          your requirements:
                                care for land
                                care for neighbor
                                care for future.

We name you king, Lord, sovereign—
    so undemocratic!
    and in naming become aware of our status
        before you . . . loved, sent, summoned.
        We pray in the name of the loved, sent, summoned Jesus.

Your New Word amid Our Anxiety

On Reading 1 Kings 2:1-9

The promises roll off your lips
    and into our ears:
  I will be with you;
  I will love you faithfully;
  I will be your God;
  My covenant is forever.

We count on your words that flow from our ears
    to our hearts, and we are glad.

But even while we listen,
    we live much of our lives underneath the table.
We read these old stories, and
    we know about intrigue and fear and
            anxiety and near violence
                and deception.
  We mostly do not act out our violence
    but we imagine and ponder and scheme;
  and then we, too, must cover up
  and the cover-up ferments;
  our lives become complex and burdened.

We keep inventing ourselves and our underneath selves turn out
    to be less than adequate
    and we wish we were other than we are.
We juggle your good purposes and
    our hidden yearnings and
    try to serve two masters,
    try to live two narratives,
    try to live two dreams,
and we are weary.

Because we know our hearts of anxiety so well,
    we seem fated to disease.
But because we know your heart of fidelity so well,
    we know you will defeat our demons
            and make us new.

We know about your abiding fidelity in
        Jesus of Nazareth.
Give us patience and steadfastness as we
            process the ragged edges of our lives.

Ourselves at the Center

On reading 2 Samuel 7

We are your people,
   mostly privileged
      competent
      entitled.
Your people who make futures for ourselves,
            seize opportunities,
            get the job done
               and move on.

In our self-confidence, we expect little
            beyond our productivity;
         we wait little for
               that which lies beyond us,
      and then settle with ourselves
            at the center.

And you, you in the midst of our privilege,
               our competence
               our entitlement.

You utter large, deep oaths
            beyond our imagined futures.
   You say—fear not, I am with you.
   You say—nothing shall separate us.
   You say—something of new heaven and new earth.
   You say—you are mine; I have called you by name.
   You say—my faithfulness will show concretely
         and will abide.

And we find our privilege eroded by your purpose,
            our competence shaken by your future,
               our entitlement unsettled by your other children.

Give us grace to hear your promises.
Give us freedom to trust your promises.
Give us patience to wait and
    humility to yield our dreamed future
        to your large purpose.

We pray in the name of Jesus who
is your deep *yes* over our lives.

Circled by Mercy

On reading 2 Samuel 11

We all know about being entitled
    and then growing careless.

We all know about self-indulgence,
      even amid work to be done.

We all know about being—for a moment—
    beyond Torah requirement and
    outside of your world of command.

We know about seasons of life not given over to us
    and grief at being failed selves.

We also know that you circle back among us
      in harshness and in mercy,
      in rigor and in generosity.

Now our world has gone careless and
        self-indulgent and
        beyond Torah.

So circle back, we pray—one more time,
    among us with your mercy,
        our only source of comfort,
        for we belong to you in your faithfulness.

We Bid Your Presence

On reading Psalm 22

We know about your presence
    that fills the world,
    that occupies our life,
    that makes our life in the world true and good.

We notice your powerful transformative presence
    in word and
    in sacrament,
    in food and in water,
    in gestures of mercy
        and practices of justice,
    in gentle neighbors
        and daring gratitude.

We count so on your presence
    and then plunge—without intending—into your absence.
    We find ourselves alone, abandoned, without resources
        remembering your goodness,
        hoping your future,
    but mired in anxiety and threat and risk beyond our coping.

In your absence we bid your presence,
    come again,
    come soon,
    come here:

Come to every garden become a jungle
Come to every community become joyless
sad and numb.

We acknowledge your dreadful absence and insist on your presence.
Come again, come soon. Come here.

Practitioners of Memos

Here we are, practitioners of memos:
    We send e-mail and we receive it,
    We copy it and forward it and save it and delete it.
    We write to move the data, and
            organize the program,
            and keep people informed—
and know and control and manage.

We write and receive one-dimensional memos,
      that are, at best, clear and unambiguous.
  And then—in breathtaking ways—you summon us to song.
  You, by your very presence, call us to lyrical voice;
  You, by your book, give us cadences of praise
    that we sing and say, "allelu, allelu."
  You, by your hymnal, give us many voices
    toward thanks and gratitude and amazement.
  You, by your betraying absence,
    call us to lament and protest and complaint.
  All our songs are toward you
    in praise, in thanks and in need.

We sing figure and image and parallel and metaphor.
We sing thickness according to our coded community.
We sing and draw close to each other, and to you.
We sing. Things become fresh. But then the moment breaks
  and we sink back into memo: "How many pages?"
                  "When is it due?"
                "Do you need footnotes?"
  We are hopelessly memo kinds of people.
  So we pray, by the power of your spirit,
    give us some song-infused days,
    deliver us from memo-dominated nights.

Give us a different rhythm,
  of dismay and promise,
  of candor and hope,
  of trusting and obeying.

Give us the courage to withstand the world of memo
  and to draw near to your craft of life
      given in the wind.
  We pray back to you the Word made flesh;
  We pray, "Come soon."
  We say, "Amen."

The World Is Not Safe

Despite (or because of) privilege, we live in
a dangerous world of brutality, force, and
threat. We are surrounded by terrorism,
war, abuse, exploitation, and death. Evil is
rampant, and fear too easily pervades.
Despair overtakes us when we realize that
our lives are not free of danger. Yet we are
not always the innocent victims. We
sometimes engage in collusion and
complicity. We might easily be called
perpetrators.

The Threat upon Us

Summertime . . . when the living is easy.

You give us summer and winter,
    cold and heat,
    seedtime and harvest,
but summer is special—
  grills and patios and pools
        and baseball.

We take our ease,
  even amid terrorism.
  The threat is mostly remote,
      and the war in Iraq (or Afghanistan or Sudan or . . .)
  scarcely calls us in our privilege to attention.

And then, right in the middle of our easy living,
  the bombs burst on the street corner,
      on the bus,
      on the train.
  the smoke, the fire, the shrieking,
  the dash of emergency vehicles,
all brought very near, all brought right up
      against our easy summer living.

We experience a sinking sense
  that the world is not safe,
  that our life is not free of threat,
  and we wonder where and when next
      will come assault on our well-arranged lives.

We turn to you, partly out of need,
  partly out of habit, partly out of trust.

We know you to be Creator, who maintains order,
Redeemer, who loves us more than we love ourselves.

But we are so self-sufficient,
we do not easily turn from our ways to yours.
And so amid our trust in you
comes our fated self-confidence,
our urge to manage,
our wish for self-sufficiency.

So we, unsettled in deep ways,
want to believe more than we do.
But even now we believe enough to know that your
good way does not depend on our trust.
So be our God—yet again—
this time, and
we will be honest in our double-mindedness
as we turn to you in our fear.

The Pulse of Anxiety
at a G-8 Conference

We loved the pageant of government!
We watched while power strutted
    and patriotism blossomed.
We remembered that "all men are created equal"
  (and wondered about those not men).
We heard cadences of "liberty and justice for all,"
  but noticed there was more talk
  about liberty than about justice.

We listened yet again to the
  sounds of terror and fear and threat,
  and imagined in this "theatre of self-confidence"
  that we could somehow make ourselves
              safe and unafraid.

Except, of course, the world is a dangerous place,
  and we have the uneasy feeling that the good
  world we have treasured is slipping through
              our fingers,
  and we feel the pulse of anxiety,
  and have waves of doubt about our official rhetoric—
  not because we are disloyal or unpatriotic,
    but because we suspect that the big rhetoric
        does not get close enough to the scars of reality.

We pause away from the ceremony,
  remember our baptism,
  and hear yet again your Lordly,
    "Do not fear."

We hear your assurance amid our anxiety.
We pray now for freedom to trust your promise,
     to turn away in the quiet of the vexed night,
          away from our missiles and our weapons
               and our violence,
          away from our global influence
               and control,
          away from our strut of superpower,
     in order to hear the fragile voice of the Easter Christ,
          "Peace I leave with you,
          my peace I give to you."
We hunch that if we trust that good word, we will be
                    less afraid,
                    less anxious,
                    less inclined to brutality,
                    and less anxious,
                         therefore more neighborly.

Loom large among us that we may be this day our best selves.

Remembering

On the anniversary of Hiroshima

It was the end of the war,
    V-E day and then V-J day,
    V-J victory over Japan,
        wrought by the bombs at Hiroshima
            and Nagasaki.

That awesome fiery cloud—
  a new mode of power in the world,
  a new capacity for destruction,
  a new means for victory and for defeat,
    an offer of security . . . and savage inhumanity.

Some remember best the relief,
    the troops coming home,
    the end of fear,
    the sober, solemn surrender on the USS Missouri.
  And just below that surface,
    some recall as well,
        the destruction and burning homes,
        the scarred children,
        the wrecked cities,
        the wounding and abiding contamination.

And now years later,
    we have learned, so it seems, so little
    after all this time,
        and still the anxious quest for security,
        still the many bombs and missiles,
            now more sophisticated, but just as lethal,
        still the anxiety for our young at war,

and still a body count of countless bodies,
and destroyed cities,
and wounded children,
and the long procession of fear and hate
and vengeance.

We learn so little so late,
remembering in the mix of pride and anxiety
of hope and some shame.

So teach us to reckon our life differently,
to count our days as gifts of your mercy,
to value our children and all the children,
to settle for less oil, and
less control, and
less force.

Finally, to cast ourselves on your fragile
gift of life.
Undo our anxiety;
undo our arrogance;
make us finally yours,
and not our own,
given over to your goodness
and not to our violent fear.

We pray in the name of Jesus who blessed the peacemakers.

Grieving Our Lost Children

Another brutality,
another school killing,
another grief beyond telling . . .
    and loss . . .
           in Colorado,
           in Wisconsin,
           among the Amish
           in Virginia.
           Where next?

We are reduced to weeping silence,
    even as we breed a violent culture,
    even as we kill the sons and daughters of
           our "enemies,"
    even as we fail to live and cherish and respect
      the forgotten of our common life.

There is no joy among us as we empty our schoolhouses;
there is no health among us as we move in fear and
    bottomless anxiety;
there is little hope among us as we fall helpless before
    the gunshot and the shriek and the blood and the panic;
we pray to you only because we do not know what else to do.
    So we pray, move powerfully in our body politic,
      move us toward peaceableness
           that does not want to hurt or to kill,
      move us toward justice
           that the troubled and the forgotten may know mercy,
      move us toward forgiveness that we
           may escape the trap of revenge.

Empower us to turn our weapons to acts of mercy,
  to turn our missiles to gestures of friendship,
  to turn our bombs to policies of reconciliation;
and while we are turning,
  hear our sadness,
  our loss,
  our bitterness.

We dare to pray our needfulness to you
  because you have been there on that
    gray Friday,
    and watched your own Son be murdered
      for "reasons of state."

Good God, do Easter!
  Here and among these families,
  here and in all our places of brutality.

Move our Easter grief now . . .
  without too much innocence—
  to your Sunday joy.
We pray in the one crucified and risen
    who is our Lord and Savior.

At the Death of a Dictator

December 10, 2006 at the death of Augusto Pinochet

Nations come and go,
empires rise and fall,
tyrants abuse and exploit,
   and death comes,
  and we ponder the limit of human power,
         the boundary of human ambition,
         the shortness of human wretchedness.

And we imagine you hidden behind
     limit and boundary and shortness,
     presiding over your promises of well-being.

In the death of Augusto Pinochet, for one,
  we saw democracy overthrown,
  constitution reduced to mockery,
  and torture and fear and anger,
  and disappearing sons and daughters,
  and silent, weeping mothers.

We know the collusion of our government
  in the authorizing of such men,
  and we are aware of our remote complicity
    in the pursuit of money and power
         at all costs.

We heard the deep, unbearable accounts
    of flesh abused,
    of bodies torn,
    of persons blanked from history
  in acts of weary cynicism and
        unbearable steel on human flesh.
In the fear and the silence and the dread,

alongside our remote complicity,
    we wonder about your hidden patience:
    why you waited,
    why you did not act,
    whether you noticed or cared.

We grasp the deep irony—
    his death juxtaposed to Advent.
    We wait for your coming as
        we mark his pitiful going,
        reduced to weakness,
            dodging indictments
            and evading conviction.

We remember him and his kind
    and dare—
        after a deep breath—
    to pray yet again for your
        coming kingdom of mercy and
                justice and
                compassion.

Come against the torture;
come against the militarism;
come against the systemic violence;
come as your true self and contradict the world
    so full of unbearable deathliness.

Come soon, come now, for we
    yearn to sing and dance.

On Peace and War

We are aware, acutely aware in your presence,
   of the grind of tanks,
   of the blast of mines hidden against human flesh,
   of the rat-tat-tat of sniper fire.

We are aware of the stench of death,
   bodies of our own military women and men,
   bodies of countless Iraqis,
     and the smell makes us shiver.

Such smells and sounds are remote from us,
   but not remote from us are bewilderment,
               and anxiety, and
               double-mindedness.

We are bewildered,
   whether we are liberators or invaders,
   whether they are terrorists or freedom fighters,
   whether we should yearn for peace or savor victory.

The world has become so strange,
   and our place in it so tenuous,
   where gray seems clearer than the white purity of our hopes,
      or the darkness of our deathly passions.
     There is so little agreement among us,
     perhaps so little truth among us,
     so little, good Lord, that we scarcely know how to pray,
         or for what to pray.

We do know, however, to whom to pray!
We pray to you, creator God, who wills the world good;
We pray to you, redeemer God, who makes all things new.

We pray to you, stirring Spirit, healer of the nations.
We pray for guidance,
And before that, we pray in repentance,
    for too much wanting the world on our own terms.

We pray for your powerful mercy,
    to put the world—and us—in a new way,
        a way after Jesus who gave himself,
        a way after Jesus who confounded the authorities and
            who lived more excellently.

Whelm us by your newness, by peace on your terms—
        the newness you have promised,
        of which we have seen glimpses in your Son
                    who is our Lord.

Victims . . . and Perpetrators

On reading Jeremiah 50–51

Mighty God, giver of Peace, slogan for war,
  We watch while cities burn and
                children cry and
                women weep.
  We listen while tanks roll and
                missiles zizzle, and
                mobs assemble.
  We smell while
        flesh burns and
        old tires smoke and
        oil wells flame
            out of control.

We dare say,
we dare imagine,
we dare confess, that yours is the Kingdom and the Power and the
  Glory.
                We come to you as victims of terror and
                  mass death.
                We come as perpetrators of death and massacre.
                We come as citizens and patriots and taxpayers
                  and parents and children.
                We come bewildered, angry, sorry.

You, you beyond the smell and the din and the smoke.
You, beyond our hopes and our hates.
You, our beginning before time
  our end beyond time.
Be present in ways we cannot imagine.
Be present—save us from our power
              save us from our violence,
              save us from our fear and hatred,

save us as only you can do.
Save us as you have before saved us . . .
in love and power
in compassion and justice
in miracle and in waiting.
Save us because we are your people
and because this is your world.

On Theodicy

On reading Psalm 145:15-16

We gladly confess:
   "The eyes of all look to you,
     and you give them their food
         in due season.
   You open your hand,
     satisfying the desire of
         every living thing."

That we gladly and confidently confess—
And yet, we notice your creatures
         not well fed
     but mired in hunger, poverty, and despair.

And yet, we notice the power of evil
     that stalks the best of us:
     the power of cancer,
     the dread of war,
     sadness of death—
         "good death"
         or cruel death.

And so we pray confidently toward you,
     but with footnotes that qualify.
  We pray confidently, but we will not deny in your
         presence the negatives that
           make us wonder.
  We pray amid our honest reservations,
     give us patience to wait,
         impatience to care,
         sadness held honestly,
         surrounded by joy over your
           coming kingdom—

and peace while we wait—
and peace at the last,
    that we may be peacemakers
        and so your children.

We pray in the name of your firstborn Son, our peacemaker.

June Loveliness Shattered

This June—like every June—
    is a fine time to be alive:
  the sun is warm, but not yet too hot;
  the light stays longer and night comes later;
  the summer eases the schedule,
    and we are taken up
        in weddings and brides,
        in proms and graduations,
        in successes and endings,
        in exciting new beginnings.

We are among the many creatures of your creation,
    who luxuriate in long days
        ready for peaceable nights;
    a great serenity comes to us,
        in sure knowledge that you govern well
          and care for us in generous ways.

Just at the cusp of night,
  for an instant the loveliness is shattered:
    there is a siren in its
      disruptive eeriness—
  happily not too close, but we do not know:
      a robbery,
      an assault,
      a heart attack,
      a scene of domestic violence,
      some shattering that sobers our ease.

We are reminded
  that the world is deep in instability,
  that the world is saturated with ready violence,

that our ease is without full guarantee,
and that death stalks close even to us.

We come to rest—torn between grateful ease
and weariness at the edge.

Just as we fall into sleep or dream or nightmare,
after the piercing siren,
we hear a bird,
a curfew against our anxiety,
a trust affirmed,
a witness to your good governance.

We fall back not fully at ease,
but confident enough to trust our
June night to your safekeeping.

We pray in the name of Jesus who walked into Saturday night
and began again at daybreak.

Christmas . . . the Very Next Day

Had we the chance, we would have rushed
    to Bethlehem
        to see this thing that had come to pass.

Had we been a day later,
    we would have found the manger empty
        and the family departed.

We would have learned that they fled to Egypt,
    warned that the baby was endangered,
    sought by the establishment of the day
      that understood how his very life
        threatened the way things are.

We would have paused at the empty stall
    and pondered how this baby
        from the very beginning was under threat.

The powers understood that his grace threatened all our
      coercions;
they understood that his truth challenged all our lies;
they understood that his power to heal
    nullified our many pathologies;
they understood that his power to forgive
    vetoed the power of guilt and
        the drama of debt among us.

From day one they pursued him,
    and schemed and conspired
      until finally . . . on a gray Friday . . .
        they got him!

No wonder the family fled, in order to give him time
for his life.

We could still pause at the empty barn—
and ponder that all our babies are under threat, all the
vulnerable who stand at risk
before predators,
our babies who face the slow erosion of consumerism,
our babies who face the reach of sexual exploitation,
our babies who face the call to war,
placed as we say, "in harm's way,"
our babies, elsewhere in the world,
who know of cold steel against soft arms
and distended bellies from lack of food;
our babies everywhere who are caught in the fearful display
of ruthless adult power.

We ponder how peculiar this baby at Bethlehem is,
summoned to save the world,
and yet
we know, how like every child, this one also was at risk.
The manger is empty a day later . . .
the father warned in a dream.
Our world is so at risk, and yet we seek after and wait for
this child named "Emmanuel."
Come be with us, you who are called "God with us."

Yom Kippur

On this day our Christian thoughts are turned
   to Jewish possibilities of forgiveness and reconciliation.
On this day we stand with them in covenant,
     before you,
     before your Torah,
     amid a world torn asunder.

Our thoughts are of death and destruction,
       of fragility and life under threat.
  We ponder cities mired in mud and
    mountains wrecked in quake;
  we notice melting ice and rising water;
  we name places of violence
    far away and close to home.

We tremble in our insecurity,
     afraid to be victim,
     but now and then noticing that we are perpetrators;
       we finance and applaud faraway violence,
       usually not naming the torn bodies or
         raped mothers or forgotten children.
We feel uneasy but not frontally guilty,
  not until we face your thoughts
      that are remote from our thoughts:
  we imagine that you think in grief and disappointment
      over the mess we have made;
  we imagine that you shudder in dismay and anger
      over the violation of your good dream;
  we imagine that you are ready to abandon us.

But we also imagine that your thoughts are interrupted
        by your own poets and prophets,
    who line out newness . . .
                new exodus,
                new covenant,
                new forgiveness,
                new life.

While we watch in our dis-ease,
    we hear Easter news again,
    and your resolve of new beginning.

And so we begin to move
        from sadness to joy,
        from hurt to dance,
        from enslavement to freedom.

And then we wait again for your wonder to become visible
    in the world of empires and colonies,
        of mudslides and torrents.

We wait. Come fully, come soon.

God's Gift in the Midst of Violence

On reading Jeremiah 20:10

The world trembles out of control.
The violence builds,
      some by terrorism,
      some by state greed
         dressed up as policy,
         violence on every side.

You, in the midst of the out-of-control violence.
   We confess you steadfast, loyal, reliable,
     but we wonder if you yourself are engaged
           in brutality.
   We confess you to be governor and ruler,
     but we wonder if you manage.

We in the midst of out-of-control violence,
      we in great faith,
      we in deep vocational call,
      we in our several anxieties.
We—alongside you—in the trembling.

This day we pray for freedom to move
        beyond fear to caring,
        beyond self to neighbor,
        beyond protection to growth.

That we may be a sign of steadfastness,
　　that anxiety may not win the day.

You are the one who said, "Do not be anxious."
And now we submit to you.

Dreams and Nightmares

On reading 1 Kings 3:5-9; 9:2-9

Last night as I lay sleeping,
   I had a dream so fair . . .
   I dreamed of the Holy City, well ordered and just.
   I dreamed of a garden of paradise,
      well-being all around and a good water supply.
   I dreamed of disarmament and forgiveness,
      and caring embrace for all those in need.
   I dreamed of a coming time when death is no more.

Last night as I lay sleeping . . .
   I had a nightmare of sins unforgiven.
   I had a nightmare of land mines still exploding
            and maimed children.
   I had a nightmare of the poor left unloved,
                  of the homeless left unnoticed,
                  of the dead left ungrieved.
   I had a nightmare of quarrels and rages
            and wars great and small.

When I awoke, I found you still to be God,
   presiding over the day and the night
      with serene sovereignty,
   for dark and light are both alike to you.

At the break of day we submit to you
         our best dreams
         and our worst nightmares,
   asking that your healing mercy should override threats,
      that your goodness will make our
            nightmares less toxic
            and our dreams more real.

Thank you for visiting us with newness
     that overrides what is old and deathly among us.
Come among us this day; dream us toward
     health and peace,
we pray in the real name of Jesus
     who exposes our fantasies.

Exile

On reading 1 & 2 Kings

Like the ancients, we know about ashes,
    and smoldering ruins,
    and collapse of dreams,
    and loss of treasure,
    and failed faith,
    and dislocation,
    and anxiety, and anger, and self-pity.
For we have watched the certitudes and
    entitlements
    of our world evaporate.

Like the ancients, we are a
    mix of perpetrators,
        knowing that we have brought this on
            ourselves, and a
            mix of victims,
                assaulted by others who rage against us.

Like the ancients, we weep in honesty
    at a world lost
    and the dread silence of your absence.
We know and keep busy in denial,
    but we know.

Like the ancients, we refuse the ashes,
    and watch for newness.
Like them, we ask,
    "Can these bones live?"

Like the ancients, we ask,
    "Is the hand of the Lord shortened,
        that the Lord cannot save?"

Like the ancients, we ask,
    "Will you at this time restore what was?"

And then we wait:
    We wait through the crackling of fire,
                        and the smash of buildings,
                        and the mounting body count,
                        and the failed fabric of
                            medicine and justice and education.
    We wait in a land of strangeness,
        but there we sing, songs of sadness,
                        songs of absence,
                        belatedly songs of praise,
                        acts of hope,
                        gestures of Easter,
                        gifts you have yet to give.

Salvation Oracles

On reading Isaiah 43:1-5

There is a long list of threats around us:
    terror,
    cancer,
    falling markets,
    killing,
    others unlike us in all their variety,
    loneliness,
    shame,
    death—
    the list goes on and we know it well.

And in the midst of threat of every kind,
    you appear among us in your full power,
        in your deep fidelity,
        in your amazing compassion.
    You speak among us the one word that could matter:
        "Do not *fear*."

And we, in our several fearfulnesses, are jarred by your utterance.
    On a good day, we know that your sovereign word is true.
    So give us good days by your rule,
        free enough to rejoice,
        open enough to change,
        trusting enough to move out of new obedience,
        grace enough to be forgiven and then to forgive.

We live by your word. Speak it to us through the night,
    that we may have many good days through your gift.

Brick Production

We need to be reminded of the ones who
lack voice or whose voice we do not
often hear. We think them unlike us,
but they are our neighbors—the widows,
the orphans, the immigrants, the poor,
the laborers, the prisoners, the slaves,
the addicts. They are the ones who dwell
in places short of mercy, absent of justice,
defaulted on the gifts of life. They
are noticed acutely by God. Are they
noticed by us?

A Prayer of Protest

Since our mothers and fathers cried out,
since you heard their cries and noticed,
since we left the brick production of Egypt,
since you foiled the production schedules of Pharaoh,
    we have known your name,
    we have sensed your passion,
    we have treasured your vision of justice.

And now we turn to you again,
    whose precious name we know.
We turn to you because there are
    still impossible production schedules,
    still exploitative systems,
    still cries of pain at injustice,
    still cheap labor that yields misery.

We turn to you in impatience and exasperation,
    wondering, "How long?" before you answer
      our pleading question,
    hear our petition,
      since you are not a labor boss and do not set wages.

We bid you, stir up those who can change things;
    do your stirring in the jaded halls of government;
    do your stirring in the cynical offices of the corporations;
    do your stirring amid the voting public too anxious to care;
    do your stirring in the church that thinks too much about
      purity and not enough about wages.

Move, as you moved in ancient Egyptian days.
Move the waters and the flocks and the herds

toward new statutes and regulations,
     new equity and good health care,
     new dignity that cannot be given on the cheap.

We have known now long since,
   that you reject *cheap grace*;
even as we now know that you reject *cheap labor*.

You, God of justice and dignity and equity,
keep the promises you bodied in Jesus,
   that the poor may be first-class members of society,
   that the needy may have good care and respect,
   that the poor earth may rejoice in well-being,
   that we may all come to Sabbath rest together,
     the owner and the worker,
     the leisure class and the labor class,
   all at peace in dignity and justice,
     not on the cheap, but good measure,
     pressed down,
     running over . . . forgiven.

Labor Day

We are again at our annual moment to honor labor,
     to remember those who do hard work,
     to recall tales of depression poverty,
     to wonder at our surging economy.
As we remember, we are aware that "labor" today
   is surrounded by hostile euphemisms . . .
     downgrading,
     outsourcing,
     minimum wage,
     401(k)s,
     all strategies to cut costs,
         with the result that laborers are put more at risk,
         all the while we indulge in endless extravagance.

We are mindful this day:
   that most hard labor in our country is performed
         by people maybe not like us,
     African Americans, Hispanics,
     other people who lack our advanced skills and connections,
         and who settle for being labor that is cheap, while
         food and housing continue to grow more expensive;

   that we are here because our mothers were in labor for us,
     loving us before we were born,
     available for inconvenience and for pain,
     and as we grew . . . for worry in the night;

   that there is other work to be done, what Jesus called,
         "my Father's work,"
     healing the sick,
     caring for the poor,
     casting out demons,
     doing the hard work of justice.

We give thanks for those who do this.

On Labor Day, with most of us so privileged
    that we do not sweat unless we
        play tennis or jog,
give us fresh perspective on our labor,
    that our lives consist in more
        than earning and eating,
        in making and selling,
    that our lives consist in the hard, urgent
        work of the neighborhood.

Empower us as you did our mothers
    that we may birth new well-being,
    that neighbors may live in justice,
    that we may know the joy of compassion,
    that overrides the drudgery of our common day.

We pray in the name of Jesus,
    from whom we know your own self-giving life,
    for we gladly confess that "no man works like him."

At the Death of Coal Miners

All our eyes and all our ears were on the reporting.
   We awaited news of the coal miners
     who were inhaling poisonous air;
   We watched and imagined grime and sweat
     and fear and suffocation;
   We watched and listened in our well-heated homes,
     made comfortable with fossil fuel.
     The furnace ran
         and we burned oil or gas—or coal.
     We burned it easily and raised the thermostat,
         never thinking that men and women die
            so that we have fossil warmth.

We watched and listened,
   and heard management
     express "regret"
         amid an ocean of safety violations.

We listened to management with which we resonate
   because we are the management class
         that thrives on cheap labor
         and that despises government regulations.

We sat comfortably in the warmth.
   The miners breathed their last,
     business went on.

There we all were together . . .
         owners,
         miners,
         and us.

We sensed, all of us together,
  that this is not right!
 The combination of death, comfort, and cynicism
  we know deeply does not compute.

We fall so short of your vision.
So we wait.
  We wait amid death.
  We wait in our comfort.
  We wait in our cynical control.
  We wait on your coming.
  We wait for the fullness of your promises
    of peace and mercy and justice and compassion.

 Come among us full of grace and truth.
 Come among us full of mercy and justice.
 Come and show your rule over us and among us,
  that our joy will not be phony,
  that our loss will not be unbearable,
  that our hope will sustain even now.
    So we wait.

Leaving That Is So Hard

It is difficult to leave home
    and, very differently,
  it is difficult to leave slavery.

It is difficult to leave home,
  but people do it.
    Graduates do it.
    Soldiers do it.
    Job seekers do it.
  We depart the comfort and familiarity and affection of home,
    but sometimes to depart to freedom, and
            new well-being, and
            fresh fulfillments of all sorts.

It is difficult to leave slavery,
  but people do it.
    Our ancient people in Egypt left Pharaoh,
    our black citizens have become free at last,
    and on a lesser scale,
      addicts of all sorts depart to freedom and new life.

But we do not want to go,
  because it is safe and familiar and protected
    to remain "under the spell" of another power.

And having left, we yearn to return . . .
  to families only to find them different and strange,
  to slaveries because freedom demands too much.

So we leave and return,
  we grow and depart home and come home again;

we choose freedom and depart, but stay enthralled
        to too many enslavements.

We confess, as we depart and return,
    that you are the God of all of our comings and goings,
      you are the one who watches our
          going out and our coming in.

For such troubles we pray your mercy,
    that we may have courage and freedom,
    and peaceable rest.
      You homemaker.
      You emancipator.
      You, God of all of our futures.
    Give us wisdom to follow where you lead us.

On Controlling Our Borders

Jesus—crucified and risen—draws us into his presence again,
    the one who had nowhere to lay his head,
        no safe place,
        no secure home,
        no passport or visa,
        no certified citizenship.

We gather around him in our safety, security, and well-being,
    and fret about "illegal immigrants."
    We fret because they are not like us
        and refuse our language.
    We worry that there are so many of them
        and their crossings do not stop.
    We are unsettled because it is our tax
        dollars that sustain them and provide services.
    We feel the hype about closing borders and heavy fines,
        because we imagine that our life is under threat.

And yet, as you know very well,
        we, all of us—early or late—are immigrants
                        from elsewhere;
        we are glad for cheap labor
                and seasonal workers
                    who do tomatoes and apples and oranges
                        to our savoring delight.
And beyond that, even while we are beset by fears
            and aware of pragmatic costs,
    we know very well that you are the God
        who welcomes strangers,
        who loves aliens and protects sojourners.

As always, we feel the tension and the slippage
  between the deep truth of our faith
    and the easier settlements of our society.

We do not ask for an easy way out,
  but for courage and honesty and faithfulness.
  Give us ease in the presence of those unlike us;
  give us generosity amid demands of those in need,
    help us to honor those who trespass
      as you forgive our trespasses.

You are the God of all forgiveness.
  By your gracious forgiveness transpose us
    into agents of your will,
      that our habits and inclinations may more closely
        follow your majestic lead, that our lives may
        joyously conform to your vision of a new world.

We pray in the name of your holy Son, even Jesus.

Prayer of the Church

In your presence and in the company of your good saints,
    we offer you our praise and thanksgiving,
    for life and for calling,
    for the joys of friendship,
    and for the burden of faith.
As we sit in the midst of your many mercies,
    we are mindful of so many of our brothers and sisters
    who dwell in places short of mercy,
        absent of justice,
        defaulted on the gifts of life.

We can recite the grocery list of needful people
    and violent places,
    but you know them all.
As you know them and we know them,
    we pledge in this company
    to take these needful people in these violent places
    as our call from you.

We are so poorly equipped for such a call.
    But you are the God who gives
        bread and wine,
        table and towel,
        book and song,
    and with them courage, freedom, and energy
        for the task to which we are unequal.

Catch us up this day into the reality of your good purpose,
    that by the time we leave each other
    we will know—
        yet again—
    that your mercy and justice and compassion
    outrun all the needs of the world.

Sign us on and bless your church,
    bless the bishops and the priests,
    bless the pastors and the elders,
    bless all the faithful in places harder than our own,
        in places of seduction like ours,
        in places of temptation we know too well.

Keep us simple and on task,
        and we will praise you by our glad obedience.

At Table . . . Flooded with Memories

Each time we come to your table,
  we sound the familiar memory,
    "prophets and apostles,
    saints and martyrs,"
  all of us gathered:
    prophets we know, who can
          muster righteous indignation,
    apostles we know, who do not mind being sent,
    even saints, we confess their
       "communion" of the living and the dead.

And then martyrs—and our throat tightens a little—
  old martyrs before lions
  recent martyrs before death squads
    and covert government actions.

Martyrs—truth-tellers—witnesses
  in dangerous places where truth is at risk
    before princes and powers and corporate wealth,
    telling your truth of goodness of mercy
        of peace and justice
        of compassion and forgiveness.

So we gather to be truth-tellers—
    timid, bewildered, reluctant,
    half ready, half asking, "What is truth?"

We ourselves stand alongside Jesus, who is the truth and the way
    and the life.

We ourselves give witness as we can, not doubting,
                                but fearful,
                                nonetheless sent.

Pondering the Small Ways

On reading Zechariah 4:10

We ponder you in your greatness.

We bless you in your wonders of creation.

We magnify you for your miracles of deliverance.

We relish the news of your gift of
   newness given us in Jesus of Nazareth.

We make our doxology as large as we can,
     in order to match your
     massive presence in the world.

But then, in slow times and in lesser venues,
   we know you to be the God of small things:
     one widow and one orphan,
     one touch of healing,
     one lunch turned to much food,
     one small temple for a small people in a small city,
     one small scroll to power the small city.

On good days we are among those,
     who do not occupy ourselves
        with things too great and too marvelous.

It is enough that short of glory and magnificence,
   you hang in to make small places your venue for governance.
We are grateful for your "tidbits"
     that bespeak life among us.

Waves of Well-Being Subverted

In your Holy Presence,
   we confess that something strange and ominous
      is happening among us,
     so strange that we cannot understand,
     so ominous that we cannot control.

We are like Dazzling David and Smooth Solomon
   who presided over social transformations
     that soon were out of hand.

We are like them as we watch wave after wave
    of new power and new money,
      while our infrastructure disintegrates,
     and the poor grow more desperate
      amid our surpluses.

We are like them as we participate in social differentiation
    of class and mass—
   we the educated, the privileged, the entitled,
     and we scarcely know or notice
       the lesser ones who remain unnamed
       and nearly invisible.

We are like them as we sort out tasks and assignments;
  we sit in our air conditioning and move paper
    but sweat only a little—
      except at leisure.
And they sweat and work and sometimes seethe,
    fearing the paper we move that disenfranchises them.

We are like Dazzling David and Smooth Solomon
   on the way in this great economy and this great church.

We are like them, grateful, but unnoticing. Sometimes we wonder
   if we will learn anything soon enough.

Good, hard, demanding, generous God:
      we do not ask to be dazzled;
      we do not ask to be made smooth in success.
   We ask rather for courage to be faithful,
      to submit our privilege and entitlement to you,
            before it is too late.

It is your holiness that subverts our best convictions,
   and so we submit to your haunting as best we can,
   haunted as was Jesus by purposes beyond his own.

On a Bold Court Ruling

(When the Supreme Court ruled against "military tribunals"
for those held at Guantanamo Bay.)

We talk easily and often of
   "liberty and justice for all."
We are very big on liberty,
   liberty to live our lives as we choose,
   liberty to make and spend our money
     as we will,
   liberty to protect our property,
     our home as our castle,
   liberty to travel and voice opinion,
   liberty to take and seize and ensure and enjoy.

We are not so zealous concerning
       "justice for all."
   Especially when it contradicts and violates our liberty.
We are uneasy about too much justice
     for those unlike us,
     for those who challenge and disagree,
     for those who impinge upon
       our language, our oil, our jobs, our money.

But on this day,
   we give you thanks for the court,
   for the history of an independent judiciary,
   for honorable and courageous judges,
     who do not distort justice,
     who do not show partiality,
     who do not accept bribes,
  but who believe in and practice the rule of law
     even against the ideological fervor of the day.

We ask for patience and gracefulness
    that we may will your generous justice
    even when it crowds our liberty.
You are the judge who rules generously
        toward those in need.

Give us energy to order our common life
      according to your merciful way . . .
    you who acquit us,
      so that none other is able to convict us.
We pray to you, judge of all the earth.

Martin Luther King Jr.

Some of us are old enough to remember
    the balcony in Memphis,
    the sanitation workers' strike,
    the shot that broke flesh,
    the loss of Martin,
        and then the mule-drawn wagon,
                and the funeral,
        and the riots, the violence, the fear,
                and the failure.

All of us know the crowd in D.C.
  and "I Have a Dream,"
  the Birmingham jail,
  the broad stream of violence,
    and his steadfast nonviolence
        in Albany and
        in Skokie and
        in Selma.

All of us know his awesome, daring speech,
    his bravery, his hope, and his generative word.
And we know the relentlessness of our government
     in pursuit of him
    and the endless surveillance and harassment
             of this drum major for justice.

At this distance, we have little access
  to how it was then concerning ambiguity
            and fear
            and reluctance
            and violence
            and injustice.

We do not doubt that you have persisted
            even beyond Martin's passion,
            even beyond Martin's brilliance,
            even beyond Martin's fidelity, and
                        his loss.

We do not doubt that through him and beyond him,
        you, holy God of the prophets,
            are still pledged to justice and
                            peace and
                            liberty for all.

We remember Martin in gratitude . . .
            and chagrin.
And we pledge, amid our stressed ambiguities,
            to dream as he did,
            to walk the walk,
            and to talk the talk of your coming kingdom.

We pledge, so sure that your truth
    will not stop its march
        until your will is done on earth as it is in heaven.

Old Stories Become New Songs

On reading 1 & 2 Samuel

We love to tell the old, old story.
We love to sing the old, old song
    of your saving deeds of mercy and
                        freedom and
                        healing and
                        newness.

We know about Exodus freedom
    and dancing tambourines.

We know about land and huge clusters of grapes.

We know about rivers of water and
                    rivers of oil.

We know about the strangeness that
        the blind see,
        the lame walk,
        the lepers are cleansed,
        the dead are raised,
        the poor rejoice.

We know. Give us courage to
trust what we know and to
obey what we hope.

We know that the old, old story—in our telling—becomes
a new, dangerous, transforming song. And so we sing!

Can We Risk It?

We have been sent dangerously by God's address—called by name, entrusted with risky words, and empowered with authority. We are to tell the truth openly, work for justice, and stand in solidarity with our neighbors. The cost is high, but the purposes are those of the Holy God.

Jolted by Address

On reading 1 Samuel 3

We are surrounded by a din of demanding voices:
> selling,
> recruiting,
> seducing,
> coercing.

We screen them out in order to maintain our sanity,
> to secure our rest.

And then, in the night, you address us,
> you call us by name,
> you entrust to us risky words,
> you empower us with authority.

But your voice is on first hearing not distinctive.

We confuse your voice with that of an old friend
> or a deep hope
> or a powerful fear
> or an ancient bias.
We hear, but we do not listen—
jolted, bewildered, resistant.

But your voice sneaks up on us:
> you address us,
> you call us by name,
> you entrust us with risky words,
> you empower us with authority.

Sometimes . . . occasionally . . . boldly . . . we answer:
"Speak, I am listening."
Then we say, "Here am I."

And listening, we are made new and sent dangerously
by your address.

When Life Crashes

We have known forever that you call to obedience,
                    that our obedience to your purposes
                        brings well-being,
                    that our departure from you may
                        bring trouble,
                    that life proceeds on a tight calculus
                        of expectation and requirement,
                    that in your awesome rule there is rigor
                        along with generosity.

We have set out to be your faithful people
and then we fall into an unintended brokenness.
    We know about alienation from you and loss;
    we know about shame before our neighbors
                and embarrassment in the family;
    we know about the will to hide and become invisible,
    and we are consumed by depths of remorse.

When we are able, we come out of hiding long enough to face you.
                    We know all the cadences of confession and
                        repentance,
                        and that we have no secrets not already
                        known to you.
                    We sense before you our deep dread of failure
                        and our last shred of innocence gone.

We ask forgiveness and wait,
    at times before your presence we wait a very long time
        as we know of your silence and absence in our bottomness.

But we know more!
We know of your unfailing love,
                your willing generosity,
                your readiness to remember our sin no more.

And so,
    after shame before neighbor,
    after embarrassment within family,
    after dread before you,
we wait and then eventually you appear,
                  you reach,
                  you speak,
                  you touch.
You give yourself to us without judgment—
        after we have judged ourselves.

You invite us to your presence,
        to the table of your feast,
        to your walk of companionship,
        to your mission of well-being.
We take timid steps toward home and are welcomed.

Now, in this hour of free-fall,
    be your good self again,
        meet us not according to our flaw
        but according to your generous self-giving:
    Be our Christmas,
        and start the world again;
    Be our Easter,
        and draw us from death to new life;
    Be our Pentecost,
        and breathe on us to begin again;
    Be your full, generous self toward us;
        we will begin again in obedience,
            and as we can obey,
        we will begin again
            in wonder, love, and joy.

Waiting and Longing

On reading Daniel

God of the seasons,
God of the years,
God of the eons,
   Alpha and Omega,
   before us and after us.

You promise and we wait:
        we wait with eager longing,
        we wait amid doubt and anxiety,
        we wait with patience thin
          and then doubt,
          and then we take life into our
                own hands.

We wait because you are the one and the only one.
We wait for your peace and your mercy,
   for your justice and your good rule.

Give us your spirit that we may wait
   obediently and with discernment,
   caringly and without passivity,
   trustingly and without cynicism,
   honestly and without utopianism.

Grant that our wait may be appropriate to your coming
    soon and very soon,
    soon and not late,
    late but not too late.

We wait while the world groans in eager longing.

In‑Between

On reading 1 Samuel 15

We find ourselves always between
    obedience to you about which we are serious and
    coveting to advance our own interests.

You command generosity,
      and we grasp in greediness.

But sometimes your commands come through to us
     as harshness and abusiveness.
     We hear you in and through our own
        sense of right
     and we obey you in ruthless ways,
        taking ourselves always to be the "good guys."

But sometimes we break from such harsh demand
       that we have inhaled too long,
       and we find ourselves gentle and forgiving,
       and worried about going soft
         on those whom you judge.

We pray then that you would be your true self
         more clearly
         and less harshly
       that we may be our true selves,
        even if we must unlearn
        something of you.

Because your commands are sturdy and
because we are tempted to live apart from you,
     we are too often conflicted.

We do not pray to be eased from our
       dis-ease,
   but only for courage and freedom
      to relearn you and
      to reimagine ourselves.
   You and us dreamed at our best . . .
      that we may be "all that we can be."

To Be Bearers of the Word

On reading 1 & 2 Kings

You we name as Lord, Sovereign, King.
You we confess governor over nations, empires, and kingdoms.
You in your holiness remain hidden,
     evoking our extravagant doxologies.

Your rule draws close and visible
   among us
   when we see new possibilities break out,
       or watch the rise and fall
         beyond explanation.

Your rule draws close when you
     dispatch prophets, messengers, and angels,
     who dare say,
        "Thus saith the Lord."

You dispatch your sovereign word through
   human utterers . . .
     preachers, poets, artists,
       various freakish dissenters
       and dreamers.

We thank you for your word of governance;
   we do not want to be addressed
     by dreams, breaks, or possibilities.
   We most certainly do not want to be
     bearers of such
       dreams, breaks, or possibilities,
   because we are mostly agents of
     steady equilibrium.

Nonetheless, we dare yearn for your
    word and occasionally utter it.
We thank you that we do not live
    in a world unaddressed.
We thank you that you are not a God unuttered.

So we pledge, as we are able,
    to listen and to speak,
    being available for your word
        that is full of grace and truth.

Giver of All Good Gifts

On reading 1 & 2 Kings

You are the God who feeds and nourishes.
You are the God who assures that we have more than enough,
   and we do not doubt that
   you satisfy the desire of every living thing.

Even in such an assurance, however,
   we scramble for more food.
   After we have filled all our baskets
            with manna,
   we seek a surplus—
     enough education to plan ahead,
     enough power to protect our supply,
     enough oil to assure that protection.

And in the midst of that
    comes your word,
   that we share bread and feed the hungry,
    even to the least and so to you.
We mostly keep our bread for ourselves,
              our neighbors,
              and our friends.

It does not occur to us often,
    to feed our enemies,
    to share your bounty with
       those who threaten us.

We do not often remember to break vicious cycles
    of hostility
        by free bread,
        by free water,
        by free wine,
        by free milk.
Until we remember that you are the giver of all good gifts,
                        ours to enjoy,
                        ours to share.

Stir us by your spirit beyond fearful accumulation
        toward outrageous generosity,
    that giving bread to others
            makes for peace,
    that giving drink to others
            makes for justice,
    that giving and sharing opens the world
        and assures abundance for all.

We pray this even as we ponder the gift of your Son
    whom we ingest as bread and wine,
        and tasting, find ourselves
                forgiven and renewed.
    Feed us till we want no more!

We Hear and Speak

On reading Jeremiah

We are a people with many words and much talk:
                              creeds and
                              ads and
                              propaganda and
                              slogans and
                              sound bytes.

We keep listening among these words for comfort,
        and we find ourselves made
                anxious by the cacophony.

And then—the din is broken;
        You speak and we enter the zone of address.
        You speak and we are called by name.
        You name and we are summoned—
                summoned, commanded, sent.

We hear and cringe and pause . . .
        overwhelmed by mandate.
We listen and you speak again:
        you utter words of presence,
                promises of protection,
                assurances of solidarity.

We breathe easier, still afraid,
        but on our way, at risk, not alone.

Give us good ears in these days,
        that we may hear the mandate
                and listen for assurance.

That even such as us may speak you well,
> you in your sovereignty,
> you in your fidelity,
> you in your sadness
>> and in your newness.

Let your word be fleshed through our tongues and
> on our lips,
> that our fleshed verbiage may truly echo
> your word made flesh via Nazareth.

Called beyond Comfort Zone

On reading Jeremiah 23

We are among your called.
   We have heard and answered your summons.
   You have addressed us in the deep
     places of our lives.
   In responsive obedience we testify,
     as we are able, to your truth as it
        concerns our common life.

We thank you for the call,
         for the burden of that call,
         for the risk that goes with it,
         for the joy of words given us
           by your growing spirit, and
         for the newness that sometimes comes
           from our word.

We have indeed been in the counsel of your
     summoning spirit,
  and so we know some truth to speak.

But we are, as well, filled with rich
     imagination of our own,
  And our imagination is sometimes
     matched and overmatched
        by our cowardice,
        by our readiness to please,
        by our quest for well-being.

We are, on most days, a hard mix
     of true prophet and wayward voice,
     a mix of your call to justice
        and our hope for *shalom*.

Here we are, as we are,
mixed but faithful,
compromised but committed,
anxious but devoted to you.

Use us and our gifts for
your newness that pushes beyond
all that we can say or imagine.
We are grateful for words given us;
we are more grateful for your word fleshed
among us.

Exposed to Mercy, Truth, and Newness

On reading Psalm 32

We begin the new week toward you,
   from whom no secret can be hid.
We have had a night,
         and a weekend,
         and a lifetime of secrets.

We have stored the usual list of secrets,
                 of acres of guilt unforgiven,
                 of desires too rich to utter.
Beyond that, we have a secret list of hurts,
   from ancient days with parents and siblings,
   from assorted bullies at playschool
       and in adult life;
     some of us overly sensitive,
       all of us grown protective
       and capable of self-pity.

Beyond that, we have a secret list of hopes,
       some selfish and some noble,
         hopes of new freedom and new reconciliation,
          of new security and new recognition,
         of doing well and being well.

We have so much to keep hidden.
And you know—
     you know because you made us and have watched us
       from the beginning;
     you know because you see us in our waking and our
       sleeping;
     you know because you love us right through,
       beyond all of our covert capacity.

And we yearn to be known—fully, without reserve by you:
So we ask on this day,
courage to match your love,
honesty to match your generosity,
self-awareness to speak into your awareness of us.

That by the time the sun sets,
we will have rent the curtain of our lives,
and let you into the center of it all,
there to abide in holy forgiveness.
We pray through your spirit of all truth
that our truth opened to your mercy may make us free.

Income Tax Day

On this day of internal revenue
    some of us are paid up,
    some of us owe,
    some of us await a refund,
    some of us have no income to tax.

But all of us are taxed,
    by war,
    by violence,
    by anxiety,
    by deathliness.

And Caesar never gives any deep tax relief.

We render to Caesar . . .
    to some it feels like a grab,
    to some it is clearly a war tax,
    to some—some few—
        it is a way to contribute to the common good.

In any case we are haunted
  by what we render to Caesar,
  by what we might render to you,
  by the way we invest our wealth and our lives,
  when what you ask is an "easy yoke":
    to do justice
    to love mercy
    to walk humbly with you.

Give us courage for your easy burden, so to live untaxed lives.

On God's New Governance

We say so easily, "Thine is the kingdom, and the power, and the
  glory."
    We rush to the next item as though
      that mantra was obvious or unimportant.
    We mouth your rule,
And then we settle back to our habitual ways,
    of initiative and control,
    of despair and resentment,
    of varying degrees of
        fatigue, or
        cynicism, or
        anxiety.

Having made the affirmation, we find ourselves still waiting,
    waiting for your fresh word,
    waiting for your powerful appearance,
    waiting for your new disclosure,
    waiting in eager longing, but
      inured to a wait that has no end.

We present ourselves to you at the break of day.
    We are here, awake, alert,
      wanting your rule to override our disorder;
      hoping for your power to check our own power,
        to overrule our disordering;
      trusting in your glory that will drive out
        our demons and silence our idols.

Yours is indeed the kingdom, the power, and the glory.
 We submit—as did he—
  to your good rule.
 Come soon, come here,
  with your lively way through our numbness.

Epiphany

The wise ones hurried from the East.
　They are the wise of the world.
　They are the ones wise in science,
　　for they read the "intelligent design" of the stars.
　They are the wise ones of the economy,
　　for they come with gold.
　They are the wise ones of politics,
　　for they sought a king.
　They are our delegates, as we stand
　　carrying all the learning of the academy,
　　　　　　　　of the market,
　　　　　　　　of the laboratory,
　　　　　　　　of the halls of power.

They came, tenaciously and eagerly and regally.
They came and bowed down before your foolishness.
They sensed the contradiction
　　　　between his vulnerability and their sagacity,
　　　　between his innocence and their calculation,
　　　　between his exposure and their many concealing
　　　　　　robes of power.

They worshiped him!
They recognized that he called into question
　　all that they treasured,
　　so they yielded their best to him,
　　　　　　their preciousness,
　　　　　　their secret potions,
　　　　　　their rich perfumes.

And we stand alongside them with
  our wealth,
  our control,
  our smarts,
  our sophistication,
  our affluence.

Give us freedom like theirs
  to yield,
  to worship,
  to adore,
  to have our lives contradicted.

Give us grace like theirs
  to embrace the foolishness of the child,
    that the first will be last and the last first,
    that the humble will be exalted and the exalted humbled,
    that we may lose the world and gain our lives.

Give us the imagination like theirs
  to go home by another route
  on the path where foolishness is wisdom
              and weakness is strength
              and poverty is wealth.

Make our new foolishness specific
  that the world might become—
      through us—new.

Holy Regime Change

On reading 1 Samuel 3:1-14

We speak easily and glibly of "regime change."
   We imagine it is some regime other than our own;
   We imagine our rightful capacity to make such change elsewhere.

But then you in Scripture,
        you making regime change,
        you overthrowing long-established priestly power;
        you moving against things holy and treasured among us;
        you causing endings that we had never thought possible;
        you making newnesses beyond our conjuring.

And just behind old Eli and his loss of regime
  comes this Other Voice from your inner circle,
    summoning to radical newness,
    summoning to "repent," and then,
    a new regime: "The Kingdom of God is at hand."

And all our old regimes—
    of heart and of mind,
    of money and of power,
    of privilege and of entitlement—
  all are in one instant placed in jeopardy.

Give to us courage to hear your summons;
Give to us freedom to relinquish old regimes that have gone stale
  in hardness and in disobedience;
Give us ease to receive new governance that reshapes everything,
      even our deep treasures.

We live by your word; we await your news,
　　but we do so tentatively, reluctantly,
　　knowing the cost to all that is settled and old.
　　　So come, Power of newness, come here, come soon.

On Pondering Laments

We celebrate your steadfast love.
We praise you for your mercy.
We count on your faithfulness.
    We celebrate and
        praise and
        count on.

And then the world does not work right.
    We find ourselves unsafe and anxious,
        caught up in greed and selfishness,
        beset by a culture of violence and threat.

We wonder about the mismatch
        between you and your creation.

Mostly we trust,
        down deep we sometimes do not.
We risk truth-telling
        about your absence and silence and withdrawal.

We do such truth-telling,
        telling it to you,
    you . . . absent, silent, withdrawn.
    You we address, you, our only hope
        in this world and in the world to come.

Swept to Big Purposes

You call and we have a vocation.
You send and we have an identity.
You accompany us and we are swept to
     big purposes:
            chosen race,
            royal priesthood,
            your own people,
            receiving mercy.

  But we, in our restlessness,
         do not want to be so peculiar.

We would rather be like the others,
         eager for their wealth
            their wisdom
            their power.
       Eager to be like them, comfortable
            beautiful
            young
            free.

We yearn to be like the others,
  and you make us odd and peculiar and different.

Grant that we may find joy in our baptism,
            freedom in our obedience,
          delight in our vocation.

The same joy, freedom, and delight
that so marked our Lord
whom we follow in oddness.

Choirs of Hope

We are a privileged people, praying at the
edge of life as an act of candor. We hope
for new life that comes as a gift. We dream
of possibility and newness—new places,
new selves, new community. In our better
moments, we aim to follow God's lead
toward justice, resurrection, and
transformation. We strive to increase those
moments as we live, love, share the Easter
joy and become bearers of hope.

A Habitat of Newness and Goodness

Through this day we have named your name in gladness,
        we have pondered the world you have
           called "good,"
        we have relished your gift and your task,
        and we have marveled in amazement,
     yet one more time,
     at the wonder of this Easter Jesus,
     who has died and is alive among us.

Now we are homeward;
  And when we arrive there,
    it will be as it was this morning,
    with anxiety and demand and conflict
          and inconvenience.
  Except that all things will be—
    yet again—made new.
          Make new by your spirit;
          make new the church where we live;
          make new the public reality of justice among us;
          make new the practice of compassion in our
            neighborhood;
          make new the surge of peace in our violent
            world;
          make new the policies of our government
            and the workings of the church.

Make new, and we will be in Easter joy
    unafraid and unweary,
    your glad people,
    carrying among us the marks of the death
        and the new life of Jesus in whose name we pray.

Children on Mother's Day

We are children today of many mothers,
    some of us grateful and glad,
    some of us cynical and defeated,
    all of us living lives that are pure gift
        from you and for you.

As we give thanks for our mothers,
  so we think of children whom you treasure
        and invite close in.
  For newborn babies arriving in these restless days,
  for children loved and lost awhile—
    Joshua, Charles, Michael, Sophie, and a world of others,
  for children born feeble and troubled
        and loved in their need,
  for children infused with napalm and
        shrapnel and hate and fire,
  for children who know the sharp edge of Pharaoh and Herod,
        and a thousand other uneasy men of force.

In the midst of this parade of innocence,
  we submit all the treasured children of the world to you,
  that they may prosper, and that we may become more fully
    your daughters and sons,
    children of your commandments,
    recipients of your gifts,
    bearers of your hope.

You have said, "Let the little children come."
Here we are—yours . . .

that we may receive your nurture

and your discipline.

Post-Election Day

You creator God
who has ordered us
in families and communities,
in clans and tribes,
in states and nations.

You creator God
who enact your governance
in ways overt and
in ways hidden.
You exercise your will for
peace and for justice and for freedom.

We give you thanks for the peaceable order of
our nation and for the chance of choosing—
all the manipulative money notwithstanding.

We pray now for new governance
that your will and purpose may prevail,
that our leaders may have a sense
of justice and goodness,
that we as citizens may care about the
public face of your purpose.

We pray in the name of Jesus who was executed
by the authorities.

Rosa Parks

Rosa is dead . . . but not forgotten!
Rosa is dead . . .
    but remembered.
    Remembered by us here as a witness to your truth.
    Remembered by those who have sat too long
                at the back of the bus,
                  and now have moved forward a couple
                     of rows but still have no free ride.
    Remembered by
               those accustomed to sitting up front,
               those who have begun repentance that is
                 still unfinished,
               those so in control that
                 relinquishment is not easy and mostly
                 done with a grudge.

Rosa is dead . . . but remembered,
  to be retold after and long among us,
      retold because the tale we tell of her
    is an item in your large story
         of freedom,
         of justice,
         of resurrection,
         of transformation,
         and finally—not too soon—forgiveness.

As we remember Rosa, we recall your big story
      in which we are situated—
    the wonder of the sea miracle,
    the miracle of homecoming from exile,
    the astonishment of Easter emancipation.

We remember the day the hills danced in resurrection
and the waters answered in new creation.

We remember . . . and so we hope,
for your new miracles so urgently awaited,
miracles of redemption and release,
of still more back-of-the-bus people
brought to newness.

We give thanks for Rosa and Martin and Nelson
and Desmond and all those who have
trusted your goodness.

Let us walk in Rosa's parade, which is a segment of your Easter
parade.
In remembering and in hoping,
open us to your new world that is coming soon—even now!

In Human Form

On reading 1 Samuel 16:11-13

You are God, high, lifted up, majestic.
As we say, "Yours is the kingdom, the power, and the glory . . .
      forever."

You are high and lifted up;
    it dazzles us that you work your will
        through human agents—
        those whom you call and choose and empower,
        even the weak, the lowly, the nobodies.

You are high and lifted up;
    it stuns us that you have worked your will
        through such human agents as David,
        the runt of his family,
        almost left behind and forgotten,
        and you called him to power and
            obedience and success.

You are high and lifted up;
    it staggers us that you have worked your will
        through this Jesus of Nazareth,
        he of no pedigree,
        he of no form or comeliness,
        he who emptied himself in obedience;
            and you have raised him to new life,
            before whom every knee shall bow.

You are high and lifted up;
    it astonishes us that you work your will
        through human agents like us,
        people of little consequence and
            limited capacity.

You call us beyond ourselves;
you send us beyond our imagination;
you empower us beyond our capacity,
    and we become your agents in the world,
        day by day doing justice and mercy and compassion.

At the end of the day we still say in astonishment,
        that you are high and lifted up and majestic.
        We are your creatures,
        and we give our life back to you,
            filled with gratitude,
                eager for the rest that only you can give.

Hearing Better Voices

On reading the prophets

We make a pause
  amid many voices—
    some innocent and some seductive,
    some violent and some coercive,
    some forgiven and genuine,
    some not.

Amid this cacophony that pulls us
    in many directions,
  we have these old voices of your prophets;
  these voices attest to
    your fierce self,
    your severe summons,
    your generous promise,
    your abiding presence.

Give us good ears,
  perchance you have a word for us tonight;
Give us grace and courage to listen,
              to answer,
              to care,
              and to rejoice,
  that we may be more fully your people.

This City . . . of God

You are the God who has set us
    in families and clans and tribes,
    in communities and finally in cities.
We give you thanks this day that you are
      Lord of this city and all cities.

We pray for this city today,
    and for Jerusalem and
          Baghdad and
          Belfast and
          a thousand other cities.

In all our cities this day
    there will be crime and sharp moneymaking
    and compassion and forgiveness, and generosity,
    and regulations about justice and injustice.

Be our God this day and prosper our city.
    We pray in the name of the one who wept over the city.

Praise in the Great Congregation

We are bold, as your creatures, to praise you.
We praise you for the gift of life,
  and for the gift of new life in Easter.
We praise you for the mystery of creation,
  as we stand in awe alongside
    all your creatures—
        zebras,
        cabbages,
        sharks,
        all the birds of the air,
        all the fish of the sea,
        all the beasts of the field.
We praise you alongside all our human cousins
  of the single family of humanity:
    Hispanics and Koreans,
    homeboys and immigrants,
    our good friends, our fearful enemies.
We praise you with full throat and glad hearts.
We praise you on this glad day.

Around the edge of our doxology are other brothers and sisters
  with whom we stand in solidarity.
  So we name them for your attention:
    the war-wounded and amputees;
    the mothers whose sons are gone but not forgotten;
    the dying who lack health care;
    the poor who eat less than we eat;
    the prisoners who have not had smart lawyers.

We look up to you in exuberance.
We look around at them and our praise is muted,
   because we wonder some about your mercy;
      we are not completely sure of your generosity.
   Our praise turns to plea:
      look upon us in our common need
            and give us life again.
            Give new life and we will recover
                  our voice of praise.

Until then, we will watch with eager longing
      and voice muted, hopeful but with those in need;
      we pray toward you but are marked by hints of absence . . .
            and we wait.

At the Baptism of Jesus

On reading John 1:29-34

We celebrate that splashing moment at the Jordan,
    less muddy than the river is now.
  John the Baptist, voice of demand and challenge,
    and Jesus submitting to him.
  John recognizes him before the rest of us do.
  He called him, "Lamb of God,
    who takes away the sin of the world."

And then he plunged him into the waters of the river.
    He is a lamb who suffers and saves;
    he loves the world;
    he addressed the skewed, distorted
        way of the world;
    he comes up out of the water and makes new.

We become aware, out of his baptism, of a new world,
                a world of grace and goodness,
                a world of freedom and opportunity,
                a world of justice and mercy and
                        forgiveness,
all from that moment of water . . . and the dove and the name
    and the power.

And we remember our own baptism
  when we were named and claimed,
    and called to newness.
In our moment of water, like his,
  our world began again:
    we are grafted to God's new governance;
    we are summoned into new obedience;
    we are rooted in fresh goodness and forgiveness.

We hear the splash of water and pause,
   and begin again . . .
         not burdened by what is old,
         not bewitched by what is failed,
         not cowed by what threatens us.
  Now is our time for newness and hope
        and love and forgiveness, and we,
        after him, reenter your newness yet again.

Epiphany

On Epiphany day,
   we are still the people walking.
  We are still people in the dark,
    and the darkness looms large around us,
    beset as we are by fear,
                anxiety,
                brutality,
                violence,
                loss—
  a dozen alienations that we cannot manage.

We are—we could be—people of your light.
  So we pray for the light of your glorious presence
      as we wait for your appearing;
    we pray for the light of your wondrous grace
      as we exhaust our coping capacity;
    we pray for your gift of newness that
      will override our weariness;
    we pray that we may see and know and hear and trust
      in your good rule.

That we may have energy, courage, and freedom to enact
    your rule all through the demands of this day.
  We submit our day to you and to your rule,
        with deep joy and high hope.

On Creation

Yours—we gladly attest—is the kingdom, the power,
                    and the glory.

Yours—we gladly assert—are the heavens and the earth.

  It is you who has made all that is,
    sun, moon, stars,
    rivers, forests, minerals,
    birds, beasts, fish—
       and us.
  We say, "in your image."

Yours the kingdom and the power and the glory—and then us.

You do not will us to be powerless either,
    so you endow us with power to work
                to rule
                to govern.
We reflect you in our working
       in our ruling
       in our governing.

Ours is the chance for justice and/or injustice
       for mercy and/or rigor
       for peace and/or war.

We grow accustomed to our power,
  sometimes absolutizing,
  and then are interrupted by the
 doxology on which we have bet everything:

Yours is the kingdom, the power, and the glory. And we are glad.

Waiting for Bread . . . and for God's Future

On reading Micah

We are strange mixtures of loss and hope.

As we are able, we submit our losses to you.
   We know about sickness and dying,
        about death and mortality,
        about failure and disappointment.
  And now for a moment we do our
       failing and our dying in your presence,
       you who attend to us in loss.

As we are able, we submit our hopes to you.
We know about self-focused fantasy
      and notions of control.
  But we also know that our futures
    are out beyond us,
       held in your good hand.

Our hopes are filled with promises of
    well-being, justice, and mercy.
Move us this day beyond our fears and anxieties
    into your land of goodness.
      We wait for your coming,
     we pray for your kingdom.
   In the meantime, give us bread for the day.

A Thousand Glad Answers

On reading Psalms

You speak words of promise,
  and we answer.
  A thousand times we answer,
        in a thousand tongues—
    we answer in hymns of praise,
    we answer in songs of thanksgiving,
    we answer in lyrics of gladness,
    we answer in candor about hurt,
    we answer in abrasive anger,
    we answer in deep abandonment.

We answer and draw close to you.
  And in answering we are changed:
    given freedom,
    come to truth,
    bound in obedience.

We answer and are yours, all yours,
    not our own,
    yours, and
        glad that we belong to
           you our faithful savior.

Water That Does
Not Come Bottled

On reading Psalm 104

Creator God, we celebrate you:
    you make springs gush forth in the valleys;
        they flow between the hills,
        giving drink to every wild animal,
        the wild asses quench their thirst.

You send rain and water the earth, it springs to growth,
    we eat and are satisfied,
    we thank you and easily push back from the table.
In our comfortable plenty,
    we notice drought here
        and famine there, the work of human hands.
    The lacks seem remote from us,
            but in solidarity we register the loss,
                and the fear,
                and the death.

We count on water and rain and growth and bread.
We count on your regularities,
    but then we look for peace but find no good,
        for a time of healing, but there is terror instead.

We do not expect failed rain,
            or failed bread,
            or failed peace,
            or failed healing.
The failure lies deep in the fabric of our common life.

We turn away from that self-destructiveness . . . back to you.
    You—Creator, beginning and end,
        first and last.

You—seedtime and harvest,
        cold and heat,
        summer and winter.
You—whose patience we try.
You—whose sovereign will for good
        overrides our capacity for self-destruction.

Look to this world of need: restore,
            recreate,
            enliven,
            give rain,
            give food,
            give peace.
For there is no other source.
None except you in your sovereign reliability.

"You" beyond Our "Weary Selves"

You God, Lord and Sovereign,
you God, lover and partner.
 You are God of all our possibilities.
  You preside over all our comings and goings,
     all our wealth and all our poverty,
     all our sickness and all our health,
     all our despair and all our hope,
     all our living and all our dying.
        And we are grateful.

You are God of all of our impossibilities.
 You have presided over the emancipations
  and healings of our mothers and fathers;
 you have presided over the wondrous transformations in our
  own lives.
 you have and will preside over those parts of our lives that
  we imagine to be closed.
       And we are grateful.

So be your true self, enacting the things impossible for us,
 that we might yet be whole among the blind who see and
      the dead who are raised;
 that we may yet witness your will for peace,
     your vision for justice,
     your vetoing all our killing fields.

At the outset of this day,
we place our lives in your strong hands.
Before the end of this day,
do newness among us in the very places where
we are tired in fear,
we are exhausted in guilt,
we are spent in anxiety.

Make all things new, we pray in the new-making name of Jesus.

Easter in the Very
Belly of Nothingness

Death will be all right for us when it comes.
   But dying is another matter—
            so slow,
            so painful,
            so humiliating.

Death will be a quick turn,
      the winking of an eye
   but dying turns and twists and waits and teases.

We have not died,
   but we know about dying:
      We watch the inching pain of cancer,
               the oozing ache of alienation,
               the tears of stored-up hurt.

We can smell the dying
      of bombs and shells
      of direct hit and collateral damage
      of napalm spread thin and even of cities turned craters
      of Agent Orange that waits years to show,
            and lives turned to empty stare.

We watch close or distant;
   we brace and stiffen
      and grow cynical or uncaring.

   And death wins—
      we, robbed of vitality, brought low by failed hope,
            lost innocence,
            emptied childhood,
            and stillness.

We keep going, but barely;
　we gather at the grave,
　　　　watching the sting and
　　　　the victory of dread.

But you stir late Saturday;
　we gather early Sunday with balm and embalming,
　　　　close to the body.
　　　　waiting for the smell but not;
　　　　dreading the withered site . . . but not;
　　　　cringing before love lost . . . but not here.

　　　　　　Not here . . . but risen,
　　　　　　　　gone,
　　　　　　　　awakened,
　　　　　　　　alive!

The new creation stirs beyond the weeping women;
　O death . . . no sting!
　O grave . . . no victory!
　O silence . . . new song!
　O dread . . . new dance!
　O tribulation . . . now overcome!

O Friday God—Easter the failed city,
　　　　　　Sunday the killing fields.
　And we, we shall dance and sing,
　　　　　　thank and praise,
　　　　into the night that holds no more darkness.

On the Oracles against the Nations

On reading Revelation 11:15

We know well the "honor roll" of nation states
                and mighty empires
    that run all the way from Egypt and Assyria to Britain and
                Japan and Russia—
                and finally us.
We know about the capacity for order that they have
    and the accompanying capacity for exploitation
    and violence.
We know that the great powers, while held in your hand,
    are tempted
        to autonomy and arrogance.

In the midst of war, we ponder modern empire. In these
    moments, we hold our own resource-devouring empire up in
    your presence. For the moment, we pray for it:
            forgiveness for its violence,
            authority for its vision of freedom,
            chastening for its distorted notion of peace.

We pray, for the moment, that our very own empire may be a
    vehicle for your good purposes. Beyond that, we pray the old
    hope of our faith:
      that the kingdoms of this world
          would become the kingdom of our God
          and of his Christ.

We do not doubt that you will reign forever and ever. Along with
all waiting powers, we sing gladly:
Forever and ever,
Hallelujah!
Hallelujah!

Prayer of Illumination

Truth-telling, wind-blowing, life-giving spirit—
  we present ourselves now
    for our instruction and guidance;
  breathe your truth among us,
      breathe your truth of deep Friday loss,
          your truth of awesome Sunday joy.

Breathe your story of death and life
  that our story may be submitted to your will for life.
We pray in the name of Jesus risen to new life—
          and him crucified.

On Leaving Bondage
. . . Yet Again

Now we depart,
   as our ancient ancestors always departed.
   We leave, some of us encouraged,
        some of us unscathed,
        some of us energized,
        all of us weary.

We leave, to depart to a better place . . .
   Home . . . where we will be welcomed
      with varying measures of
         eagerness,
         resentment,
         responsiveness, or
         anxiety.

We pray for good departures,
   in the way our ancestors left Egypt,
      that we may leave the grind of productivity,
        and the hunger of craven ambition,
      that we may leave for a place of wondrous promise,
        visited en route by bread from heaven
        and water from rocks.

We pray for big departures, like those of our ancient parents,
      that we may leave where we have been and
        how we have been and
        who we have been.

To follow your better lead for us,
   you who gives new place,
      new mode,
      new self.

We pray, each of us, to travel in mercy,
   that we be on our way rejoicing,
     arriving in wonder, love, and praise.